AF083716

Bristol Lodekka

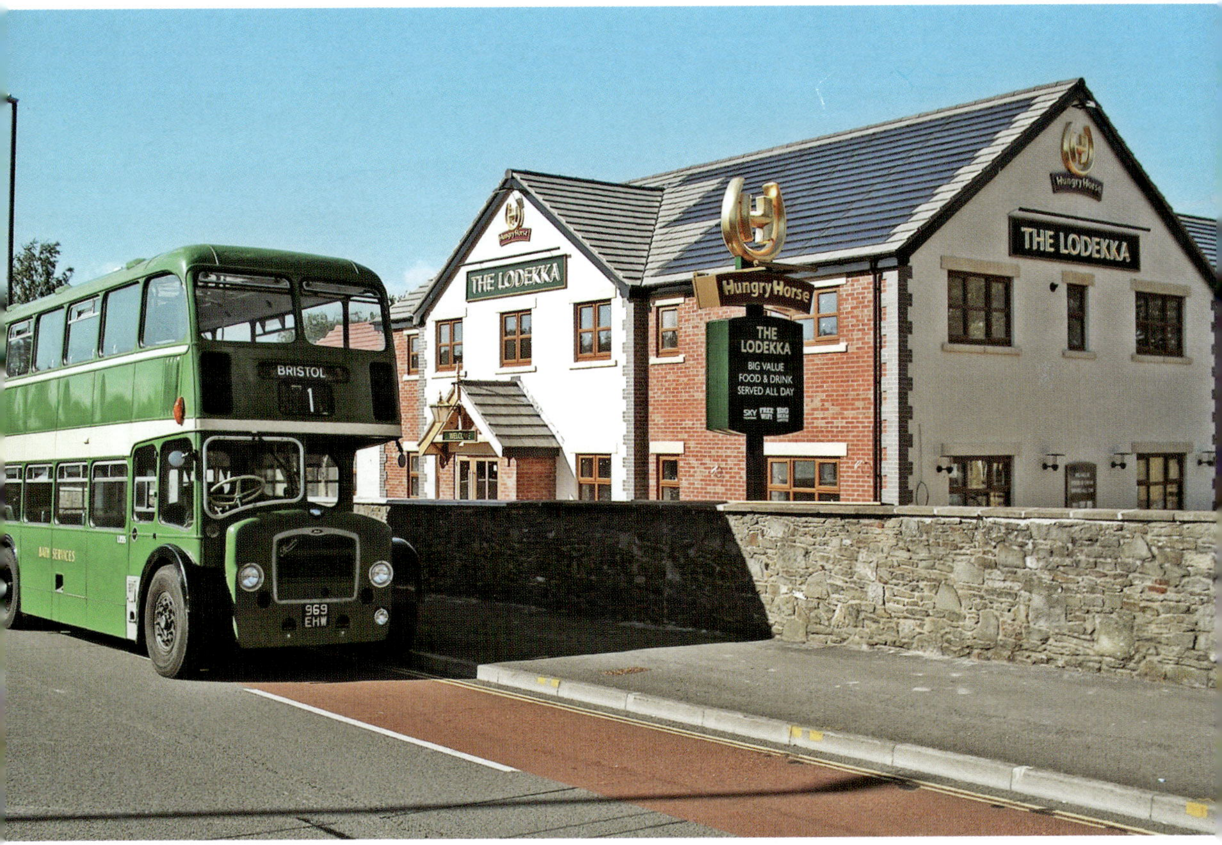

MARTIN S. CURTIS

KEY Books

BRITAIN'S BUSES SERIES, VOLUME 3

Title page image: During August 2013, a new pub and restaurant appeared on part of the site once occupied by Bristol Commercial Vehicles' Bath Road premises. Most appropriately it is named 'The Lodekka' as a tribute to Bristol's most famous bus type, being seen here prior to opening, with preserved Bath Services LD Lodekka L8515 (969 EHW) posed alongside. (M. S. Curtis)

Front cover image: Western SMT FLF6Gs, No B1933 (XCS 954) being pursued by No B1797 (VCS 351). (MSC collection)

Back cover image: Southern Vectis FS6G No 565 (TDL 998) passing through Sandown. (MSC collection)

First published in 2014 as *Bristol Lodekka in Colour* by Ian Allan.

This edition published in 2020 by Key Books.
An imprint of Key Publishing Ltd
PO Box 100
Stamford
Lincs PE19 1XQ

www.keypublishing.com

The right of Martin S. Curtis to be identified as the author of this book has been asserted in accordance with the Copyright, Designs and Patents Act 1988 Sections 77 and 78.

Copyright © Ian Allan, 2014

ISBN 978 1 913870 07 2

All rights reserved. Reproduction in whole or in part in any form whatsoever or by any means is strictly prohibited without the prior permission of the Publisher.

The Individual photographers are credited alongside each image where they are known.

Typeset by SJmagic DESIGN SERVICES, India.

Acknowledgements
I am always very grateful to the many friends and enthusiasts who make it possible to prepare a book such as this. All photographs are credited individually, but in addition I should like to thank Simon Butler, Allen Janes, Graham Jones, Allan Macfarlane, Kevin McCormack, Phil Sposito, Chris Stewart, Mike Walker and Robin Wilding for assistance in sourcing additional pictures and information. Staff at Bristol Record Office and the M-Shed museum at Bristol Docks have also been most helpful in making available records and illustrations.

Early Lodekka front cowls were produced in either metal or fibreglass until the latter material became standard. United Counties 948 (LFW 320) had been new as Lincolnshire 2312 in 1955 but was transferred to United Counties in 1971. It is seen in Bedford. (MSC collection)

Introduction

The publication in 2009 of *Bristol Lodekka* was greeted enthusiastically and appears to have reawakened an interest for many in this type of bus, which was once familiar throughout Britain. As is so often the case with such publications, much of the photographic material available could not be included owing to space constraints, but interest from readers prompted a request from the publisher to follow the original book with a pictorial colour album illustrating further examples of the Lodekka model. Moreover, one or two additional pieces of information have come to light following publication of the original volume, so despite the description of this volume as *Bristol Lodekka in Colour*, the inclusion of a small number of monochrome views was felt to be justified in order to allow still more information to be published about the Lodekka during its production years – including hitherto lost official views, never previously published.

Lodekkas first appeared in service during a period when the passenger-transport industry was enjoying a peak in popularity. Passenger numbers were among their highest ever in the provinces, and most members of society relied on public transport for journeys to and from work or school or for leisure activities. Widespread private car ownership and television in every household were both still a few years away, with the result that almost everyone used the bus!

The Lodekka was supplied only to state-owned transport operators, as a result of sales restrictions imposed on the manufacturer, yet some 5,217 examples were built between 1949 and 1968, making it one of the most familiar British double-deck bus types throughout the 1950s, '60s and '70s. All were bodied by Eastern Coach Works, of Lowestoft, a sister company to chassis manufacturer Bristol Tramways & Carriage Co, whose bus-building activities were from 1955 assumed by Bristol Commercial Vehicles Ltd. Lodekka power was usually provided either by Gardner or by Bristol's own diesel engines, although a few of the later examples received Leyland units, and the basic chassis type designation was followed by a suffix to denote engine manufacturer and number of cylinders, such as '6G' in the case of a Gardner 6LW engine.

The Lodekka introduced low-height double-deck bodywork incorporating forward-facing seating with central gangways on both decks – something not previously possible. The lower-deck saloon could also be reached from the entrance platform without the need to step up into this area, easing access for the elderly and infirm and speeding passenger movement generally inside the bus. These features were highly desirable for busy services passing under railway bridges and other obstructions, which at that time remained widespread.

Following the construction of two prototypes, in 1949 and 1950 respectively, thorough testing of the design took place before a production version was finalised. Several changes to the transmission to allow a low centre gangway on the lower deck occurred during this process. Vehicle size also increased slightly, reflecting a relaxation in permitted maximum vehicle dimensions, while an enclosed radiator was also adopted, offering a more fashionable, modern appearance. Full production of LD types (as they became known) commenced in earnest from the end of 1953. All were of rear-entrance layout, although some were fitted with platform doors, depending on their operators' requirements and the nature of their services; indeed, a number of companies retained open platforms for city and town services while specifying platform doors for buses intended for longer rural routes.

The Lodekka design represented a major advance over previous bus chassis of all makes and set standards that other manufacturers struggled to match. A flat-floor version, available in two lengths and with the choice of rear or forward entrance, appeared from the late 1950s. With air suspension added at the rear, Bristol further pushed the boundaries of this highly advanced design. Later still, Lodekkas continued to incorporate more modern features including some with semi-automatic rather than constant-mesh ('crash') transmission, and extended bodywork to increase capacity.

Having been further refined and developed over the preceding decade, production finally ceased in 1968, the Lodekka having gradually been replaced by Bristol's rear-engined VR model which – unlike the Lodekka – was suitable for one-man operation. The ability to operate double-deck buses without a conductor was something several other manufacturers had already achieved with their own suitable designs, saving both staff costs and helping to address the severe staff shortages which by then were making themselves felt throughout the bus industry. A low entrance and floor, combined with reduced overall height, was still far from universal, however.

During their production years, Lodekkas had remained tantalisingly out of reach for bus operators outside of the state-owned sector, which resulted in Dennis Bros of Guildford producing the model under licence, as the Loline, for sale on the open market. Altogether 280 Loline chassis were produced – some assembled using Bristol parts – and, whilst this was a modest number compared to Bristol Lodekka production, it enabled the design to be employed more widely by operators in the UK, while one example was even exported to Hong Kong. Indeed, Bristol Lodekkas were themselves to be found overseas in later years, many having been exported for further service at the end of their operational lives in Britain.

Even without the inclusion of Dennis Loline customers, the state-owned sector of the bus industry comprised a large number of territorial bus-operating companies, each having its own distinctive livery. Those in England and Wales were members of the Tilling group, and, whilst most had adopted rich Tilling red or green, many more carried other shades. All Tilling fleets incorporated cream relief, however. In Scotland still more variety could be found, offering a vast range of colours and styles for Bristol Lodekkas. From 1972 – by which time the National Bus Company had succeeded the Tilling group in England and Wales (and gained former BET companies, some of which had purchased Dennis Lolines) – poorer-quality poppy-red or leaf-green paint, applied to a rigid style, began to appear. Thereafter cities, districts or regions previously associated with particular colour buses began to lose their individual identities, and the majority of Lodekkas would remain in service long enough to be affected by this change. It is appropriate, therefore, that this volume recalls not only a period when Bristol Lodekkas formed the mainstay of many provincial bus fleets but also one in which company liveries were closely associated with specific areas of the country. I hope you enjoy it.

Martin S. Curtis FCILT, M Inst TA
Saltford, Bristol
August 2013

Bristol Lodekka

The first Bristol Lodekka prototype, LDX.001, appeared in 1949. Registered LHY 949, it was allocated Bristol Tramways fleet number C5000 and was tested extensively by the Bristol company and other operators. In January 1951 it was loaned to Western National, and is viewed while standing at the Saltash Passage terminus of Plymouth service 95, with Brunel's Royal Albert Bridge spanning the River Tamar behind. (R. B. Lillicrap)

Colour pictures of the first LDX prototype are extremely rare, as are rear views. Combining the two is this photograph of LHY 949 towards the end of its life, by now numbered LC5000 and displaying the short-lived gold-block BRISTOL fleetname. It was withdrawn from service in 1963 and, tragically, scrapped. (Geoff Gould)

ABOVE The second prototype Lodekka, featuring a revised driveline and deeper windows, was built in 1950 and joined West Yorkshire Road Car as its 822 (JWT 712). The close collaboration between Bristol Tramways and Eastern Coach Works was a crucial factor in the Lodekka's revolutionary design, which might have swept away double-deckers with side upper-deck gangways, but unfortunately, as state-owned manufacturers, both companies were restricted to supplying customers in the nationalised sector. (ECW)

RIGHT After thorough testing of the prototypes a batch of six pre-production LD-type Lodekkas was produced during 1953. These were very different in appearance, featuring a cowl to conceal the radiator, and at 8ft wide by 27ft long were slightly larger, reflecting changes in maximum permitted vehicle dimensions. Among them was Hants & Dorset 1337 (LRU 67), seen in later guise as 1401 at Bournemouth during the summer of 1975, by which time it was 22 years old. (M. S. Curtis)

Bristol Lodekka

ABOVE Full production of Lodekkas commenced late in 1953, by which time a backlog of orders had to be fulfilled. Cumberland 361 (ORM 143) shows the original appearance of production LD Lodekkas, with a slatted grille and a slightly lower bonnet line than that of the pre-production vehicles. Deep front wings extended almost to the foot of the cowl, although in due course these would be modified by most operators. Seating was provided for 60 passengers. (P. Hulin)

OPPOSITE TOP No colour photographs have been found of the red Lodekkas new to Westcliff-on-Sea, which were very soon absorbed into the Eastern National fleet (and repainted green). Westcliff was another early recipient of Lodekkas; 4228 (XVX 27), a Gardner 5LW-powered bus, is recorded as having cost £2,214 16s 10d when new in 1954. (Essex Bus Enthusiasts' Group)

OPPOSITE BOTTOM As indicated by its fleet number, Red & White L253 (LAX 625) was the Chepstow-based company's second Lodekka of 1953. Fitted with the more powerful Gardner 6LW engine, it could accommodate 58 seated passengers, with luggage space over the rear wheel arches. Sliding platform doors (operated manually by the conductor) provided an enclosed platform, despite the unusual full-height handrail. (Ken Jubb)

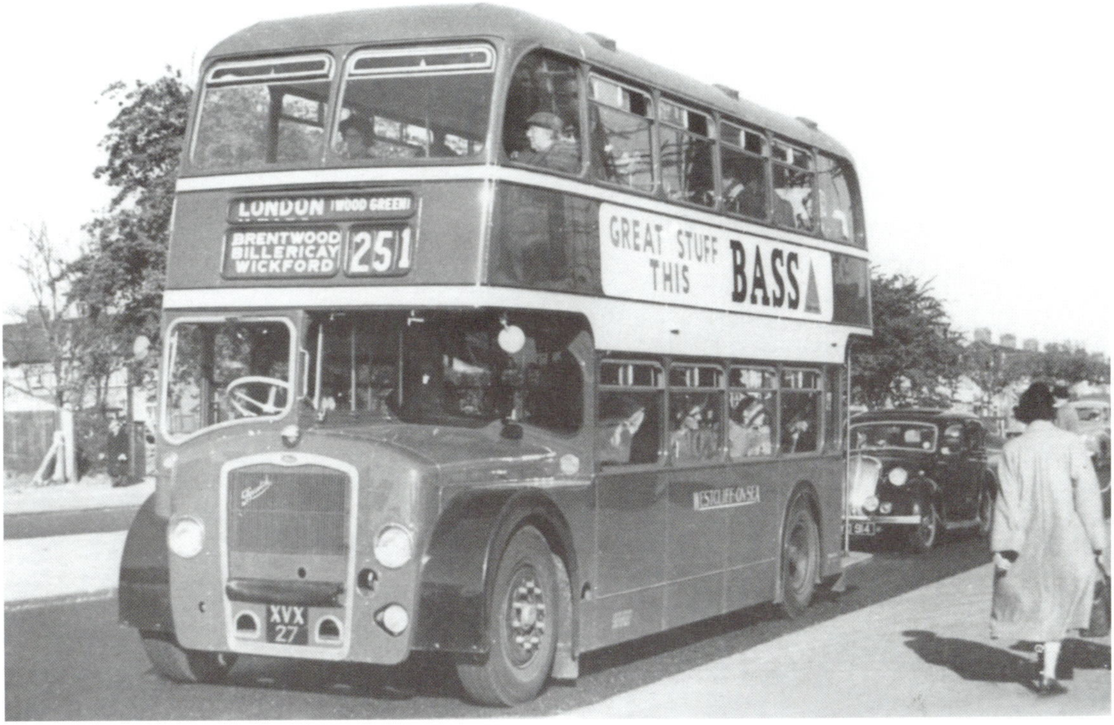
LONDON (WOOD GREEN)
BRENTWOOD
BILLERICAY
WICKFORD
251
GREAT STUFF THIS BASS
WESTCLIFF-ON-SEA
XVX 27

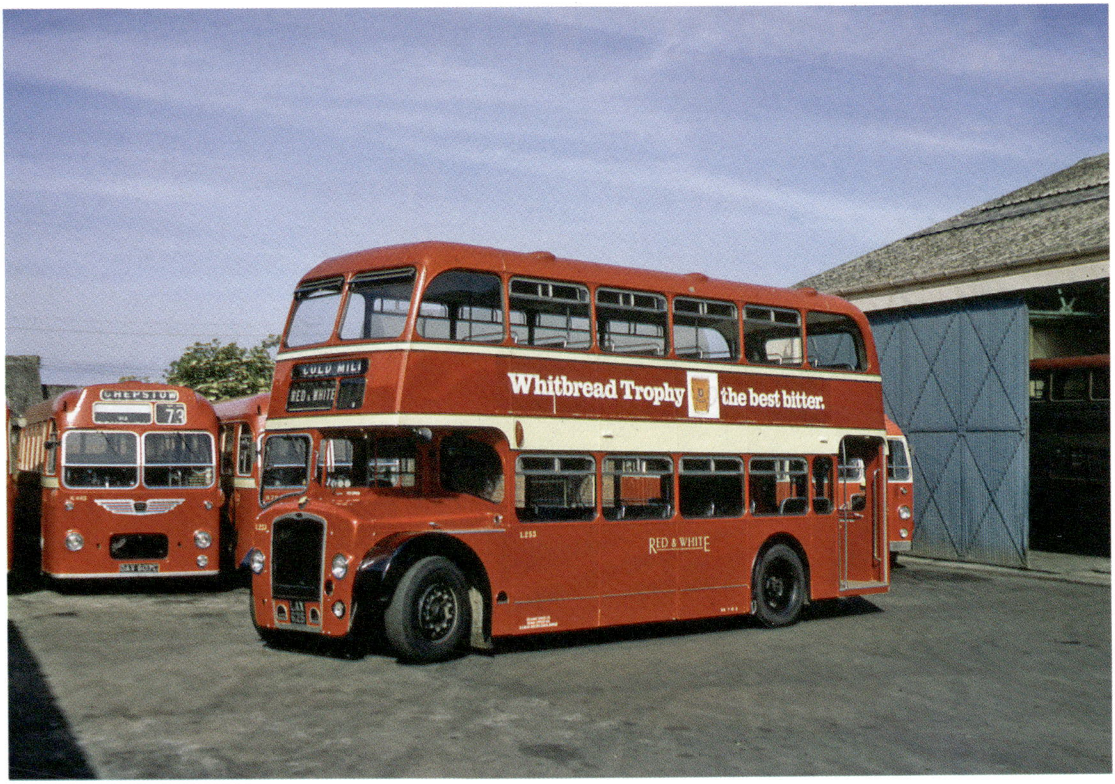
CHEPSTOW
73
COLD MILL
RED & WHITE
Whitbread Trophy the best bitter.
RED & WHITE
L253

Western SMT became the first Lodekka customer in Scotland when, late in 1954, it took delivery of B1151 (GCS 237). This was powered by a Gardner 6LW engine – resulting in the chassis designation LD6G – and was fitted with a five-speed gearbox. Seating was provided for 58. (Phil Sposito collection)

Eastern Coach Works' local operator was Eastern Counties, which took delivery of this LD5G during the first months of Lodekka production. As LKD228 (OVF 228) it received standard Tilling red and cream. (Phil Sposito collection)

Bristol Lodekka

From the mid-1950s a shallower grille design replaced the original, deep version (and was soon followed by reduced-depth front wings). Midland General 448 (XNU 432), an LD6G built in 1955, displays the revised style as it leaves Alfreton bus station during the summer of 1960. (Phil Sposito collection)

Bristol Lodekka

Its crew distracted by something alongside the quay at picturesque Dartmouth, Western National 1928 (UOD 482) awaits its next journey to nearby Townstal in 1967. This vehicle was powered by a Bristol AVW engine, resulting in the chassis designation LD6B. (MSC collection)

ABOVE The closely associated Western and Southern National fleets were eventually merged under the Western National title. With Southern National fleetnames but displaying a Western National blind, LD6B No 1874 (OTT 47) illustrates one of a number of rear lower deck window designs whilst also displaying the stepless entry from the platform to the lower saloon – one of the features which made Lodekkas so easy for passengers to use, compared with other designs of the period. (MSC collection)

OPPOSITE TOP Tilling red and cream adorned United Welsh buses, a company which was absorbed into the state-owned Tilling group as part of the purchase of Red & White's interests by the British Transport Commission in 1950. Thereafter ECW-bodied Bristol vehicles entered the fleet, among them these LD6G Lodekkas, numbered 314 (OCY 961) left, new in 1958 and 307 (OCY 954) delivered the previous year. (MSC collection)

OPPOSITE BOTTOM Durham District Services was formed in 1950 to consolidate a number of newly nationalised bus undertakings in the North East, under the overall control of United Automobile Services. Bristol buses began to arrive shortly afterwards, DBL8 (991 EHN), an LD6B with 60-seat bodywork, being added to the fleet in 1958. (Ken Jubb)

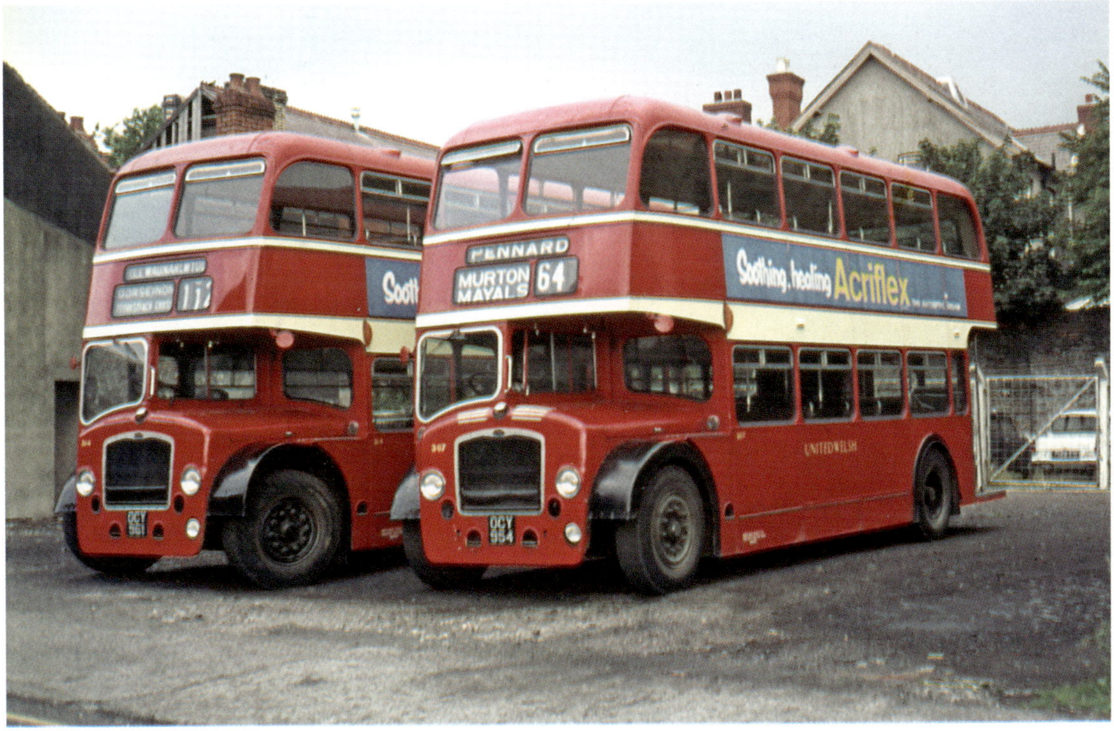
PENNARD
MURTON MAYALS 64
Soothing, healing Acriflex
UNITEDWELSH
OCY 961
OCY 954

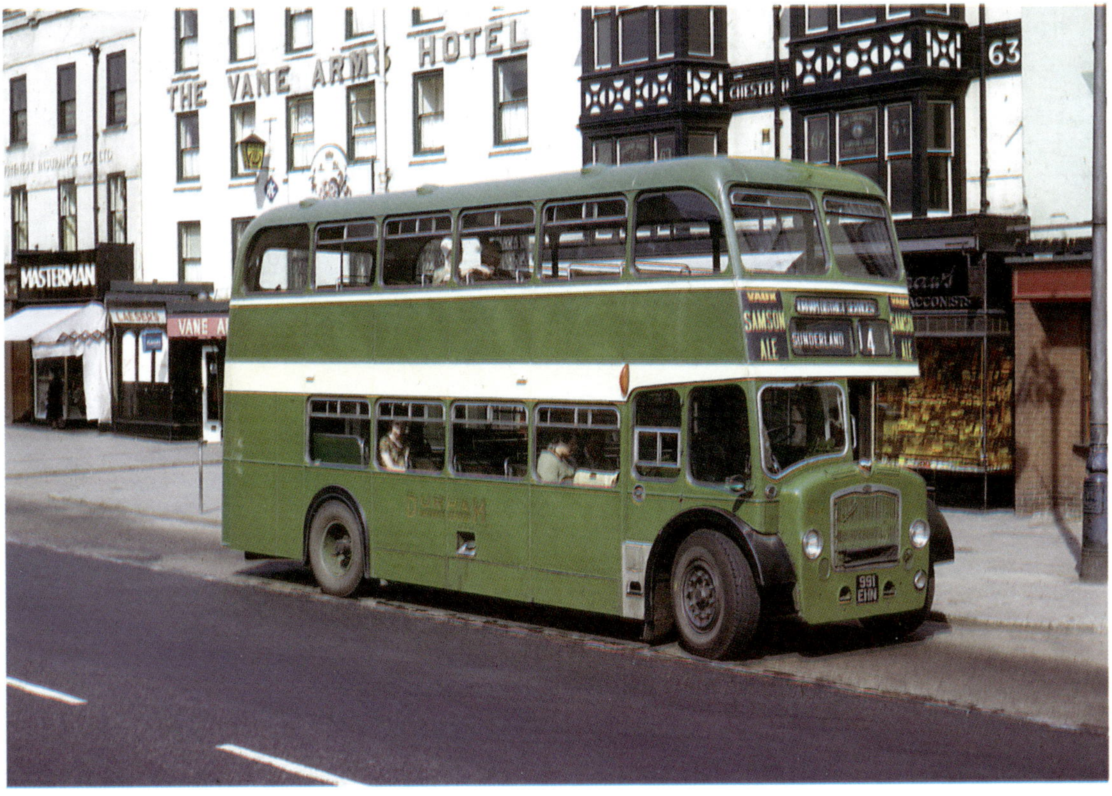
THE VANE ARMS HOTEL
MASTERMAN
VANE A
63
SAMSON ALE
SUNDERLAND 14

Bristol Lodekka

The buses of David Lawson Ltd of Kirkintilloch wore a red livery, in contrast to the blue of parent company W. Alexander & Sons. With cream wheels, ornate lining and painted advertising areas, together with 'triangular' destination displays, these – like many Scottish buses of the period – retained an elegance not found south of the border. RD20 (GWG 996) was new in 1956 and had a 60-seat, open-platform ECW body. (Phil Sposito collection)

The vehicles of Scottish Omnibuses were finished in a particularly attractive livery of two-tone green and cream which included the SMT (Scottish Motor Traction) diamond device on each side. Here 1957 LD6G No AA605 (OWS 605) prepares to turn left as it approaches its Glasgow destination. (Phil Sposito collection)

Another Scottish operator to be drawn into the nationalised sector was Baxters of Airdrie, which was acquired by Scottish Omnibuses during 1962. Baxters' colours of blue and light grey survived, however, on buses based at Victoria garage in Airdrie, among them Lodekka AA614 (OWS 614), seen here in August 1975. (M. S. Curtis)

Thames Valley 752 (MBL 833) stands outside Reading station before departing for Maidenhead. This 1956 LD6G, with coach seating, was notable as one of a number of Thames Valley buses involved in trials with reflective number plates, conducted from 1964 by the Transport & Road Research Laboratory. Three years would elapse before these black-on-white plates were introduced generally, and the buses involved in the trials carried certificates in order that drivers could, if required, confirm Ministry approval had been granted to display the registration number in what was then an unfamiliar style. (MSC collection)

Bristol Lodekka

With increased permitted lengths of double deck buses now established, Bristol Commercial Vehicles built six 30ft-long LDL-type Lodekkas for trials in 1957. Each seated 70 passengers (10 more than was possible in a standard LD), and all were Gardner 6LW-powered. They were distributed among various operators, two being allocated to Western/Southern National as 1935/6 (VDV 752/3). In the early 1970s both were converted to open-top configuration, in which form they survive today. Shortly after conversion 1935 is seen looking resplendent outside Falmouth bus station, having been named Admiral Boscawen. (Western National)

Bristol Tramways/Omnibus continued to display the Bristol coat of arms on its vehicles until 1961. This appeared throughout the company's vast operating area, being seen well beyond Bristol itself, where the Corporation held a 50% stake in the city's bus services. Here 1959 LD6G L8498 (858 CHU) awaits departure for Cheltenham from Swindon's Regent Circus while also displaying its 'T' type destination display and cast fleet-number plates, both new features at the time. (Phil Sposito collection)

When the Cheltenham District Traction Co was nationalised in 1950, control passed to Bristol Tramways, and although Bristol-built vehicles soon joined the fleet its distinctive livery of dark red and cream was retained. New in 1956 was WHY 945, an LD6G Lodekka, originally allocated fleet number L94 but renumbered L8565 in the Bristol company's series by the time this picture was taken 12 years later. (MSC collection)

Bristol Lodekka

From 1964 Scottish Omnibuses changed its livery from light green to a darker green and cream. Still wearing the lighter shade, with Scottish fleetnames, Bristol LD No AA748 (SWS 748) departs Edinburgh's St Andrew Square bus station for Glasgow, the new colours being shown by Bristol LS coach No A25 (LSC 85) alongside. (G. Lumb)

Effectively Tilling green, albeit known as 'Lothian green' north of the border, which was beyond Tilling territory, the darker shade was accompanied by a new fleetname, Eastern Scottish. Bristol LD No AA845 (WSC 845) displays the revised appearance as it arrives at St Andrew Square, Edinburgh, pursued by similar AA733 (SWS 733) on driver-training duty. (Phil Sposito collection)

In 1958 Bristol revealed an improved version of the Lodekka, incorporating a completely flat lower-deck floor, eliminating the slightly sunken gangway found on the LD model. Two further LDX prototypes were constructed, which also featured air suspension at the rear. From this point long (30ft) and short (27ft) versions of the design would be offered, initially as type LDL or LDS. LDX.003, built to the shorter LDS length, became Crosville DLG949 (285 HFM), captured here in Liverpool during May 1974. Cave-Browne-Cave heating was included, with radiators alongside the destination display. This rendered a conventional grille unnecessary, resulting in a blank cowl which was widely disliked, and few further Lodekkas perpetuated this appearance. (MSC collection)

Bristol Lodekka

By the end of 1959 the designations FS (short) and FL (long) had been adopted for flat-floor Lodekkas, while two further variants, with forward entrances, had been added, as the FSF and FLF. A pair of forward-entrance prototypes was produced in 1959, one being allocated to the Bristol operating company and the other to West Yorkshire Road Car Co. The FSF prototype was YWW 77, new as West Yorkshire DX82 but seen here as United Automobile Services L56 following its exchange for a rear-entrance FS new to United. When built it had featured a sliding entrance door, but this was soon replaced by folding jack-knife doors. (Ken Jubb)

Bristol Lodekka

Another experimental FLF was based on chassis No 169.001, which was initially allocated to Bristol's experimental department with an incomplete body, painted Tilling red. It could often be seen outside BCV's Bath Road works but after seven years was brought up to service standards and sold to Eastern Counties in 1967 as its FLF348. Registered LAH 448E, it is seen on a Norwich local service some years later, having been renumbered FLF429 and wearing NBC poppy red. It displays some evidence of its earlier role, having a non-standard air scoop running along most of its roof. (MSC collection)

New in 1960, Brighton Hove & District Bristol FS6B No 11 (RPN 11) was fitted with convertible-open-top bodywork and accordingly finished in cream livery. Here, renumbered 2011 following takeover by Southdown, it displays a number of characteristics unique to BH&D, including a split-level platform (allowing a lower entry level followed by a further shallow step for passengers boarding on the left), a route-number box over the platform, London-style running-number holders (alongside the fleet number) and louvres over the sliding side windows. (Ken Jubb)

Crosville's LD coaches, with unusual straight staircases at the rear, were originally painted all-over cream. They later received a revised livery, as shown, with cream areas reduced and green added. No DLB679 (RFM 424) has also been further modified, having lost its original deep grille and its coach blinds, the latter replaced by side-by-side destination equipment. (G. Lumb)

Bristol Lodekka

LEFT The Scottish Bus Group continued to purchase LD-type Lodekkas much later than operators in England and Wales, which instead preferred to introduce completely flat-floor F-series chassis. Pictured heading through woodland en route to Carlisle, Western SMT No B1640 (RAG 406) was among the last LDs built, in 1961. (John May)

ABOVE Southern Vectis, the principal bus company on the Isle of Wight, was well known as an operator of Bristol vehicles. FS6G No 565 (TDL 998) was recorded passing through Sandown during June 1963, when still only three years old. FS-type Lodekkas could be distinguished from LDs by their longer window bays and step position alongside the front numberplate. (MSC collection)

ABOVE The 30ft-long FL model was similar in appearance to the earlier LDL trial buses of 1957, albeit built to a slighter longer wheelbase. This Scottish example was one of a pair to enter service with Western SMT in 1961. Registered RAG 389, it was numbered B1623 and in this photograph has clearly been fitted with an older three-piece cowl from an earlier Lodekka. (Ken Jubb)

RIGHT West Yorkshire favoured the shorter, rear-platform FS model, represented here by FS6B No YDX90 (2224 WW) from the York-West Yorkshire fleet, operating in its home city. By now Bristol-engined vehicles were being fitted with the more powerful BVW unit, while standard radiator grilles were provided even when Cave-Browne-Cave heating was installed. (John May)

Bristol Lodekka

In 1961 Bristol Omnibus took delivery of four FS6Gs with 60-seat convertible-open-top ECW bodywork, for use at Weston-super-Mare. Seen in 'as delivered' condition, with gold-block fleetnames, 8578 (868 NHT) works a Weston town service with roof in position. (John May)

During their early lives at Weston the FS open-toppers carried exclusive advertising for Campbell's 'White Funnel' paddle-steamers which plied the Bristol Channel. With roof removed, L8576 (866 NHT) – an 'L' prefix (for low-height) having now been added – takes on passengers for Uphill on Weston's seafront service 103. It may be noted that, on these buses only, the Bristol fleetname was replaced in 1965 by the Weston borough arms. (MSC collection)

By 1961 it had been decided that the appearance of the Bristol Lodekka should be modernised, and consideration was given to a new design of front cowl. This recently discovered view shows a mock-up of a proposed alternative. The vehicle is a Bristol Omnibus FLF fitted with a mock cowl and bonnet incorporating elaborate grilles and light surrounds. Just visible on the lower edge is a tiny badge which reads 'LODEKKA', while the mudguards have extensions that reinstate the deeper style. The bonnet itself is significantly wider, bringing the side-lights onto the cowl rather than located on the cab front and nearside bulkhead near the entrance door. Clearly the photograph has been further modified, rather crudely, with pen and ink, to reposition the winged motif. (Bristol Commercial Vehicles)

A further proposal, very much closer to the style eventually adopted, is seen on the drive at BCV's Bath Road works, attached to Bristol Omnibus LD No LC8520 (974 EHW), which had been borrowed from nearby Brislington depot. Once again the mudguards have been extended, while a new cowl has been fitted with an attractive new design of fine-mesh grille with Bristol scrolls at the top and at 45° across the upper left corner, and 'Lodekka' appears within the bottom edge of the grille outline. The original bonnet line has been left untouched, although the rake of this new structure is slightly more pronounced than would be the case with the final version. (Bristol Commercial Vehicles)

ABOVE A group of Alexander (Midland) FLFs, among them MRD189/90 (AMS 7/8B), illustrate the new-style front cowl and deeper wings, as introduced from 1962. All had Gardner engines and 70-seat Eastern Coach Works bodies. By this time all Tilling and most Scottish operators favoured cream window rubbers, which complemented the cream paintwork, enhancing the appearance of these vehicles. (MSC collection)

OPPOSITE TOP Western SMT was unusual in retaining black window rubbers, as apparent from this view of two FLF6Gs, B1933 (XCS 954) being pursued by B1797 (VCS 351). As may be seen on the former, in addition to the fleet number and manufacturer's letter (B – Bristol), further letters and numbers were displayed on the body to indicate the year of manufacture (B4 – 1964) and garage code (G – Greenock). (MSC collection)

OPPOSITE BOTTOM Bristol Lodekkas could be found hard at work throughout Britain, from the north of Scotland to the tip of Cornwall. The latter was served by Western National, which operator's 70-seat FLF6G No 2007 (812 KDV) was captured during August 1963 when only a few months old, descending Market Jew Street, Penzance, en route for St Ives. Again, the cream window rubbers enhance an established classic livery style. (Phil Sposito collection)

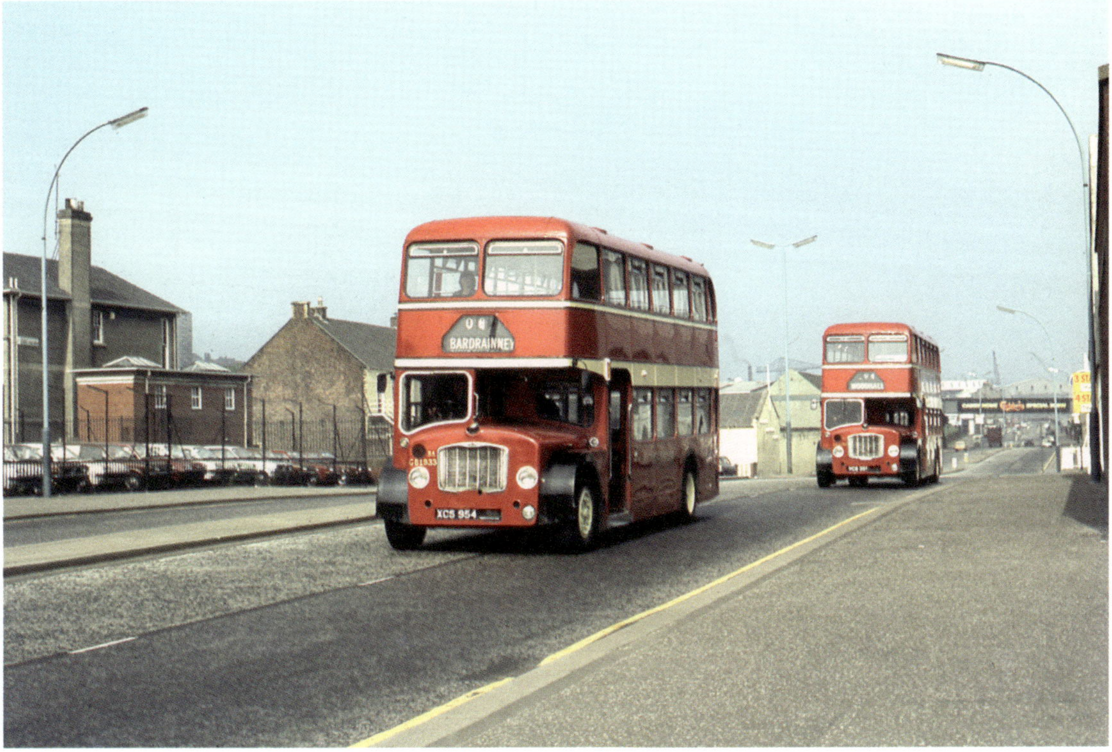
BARDRAINNEY
XCS 954

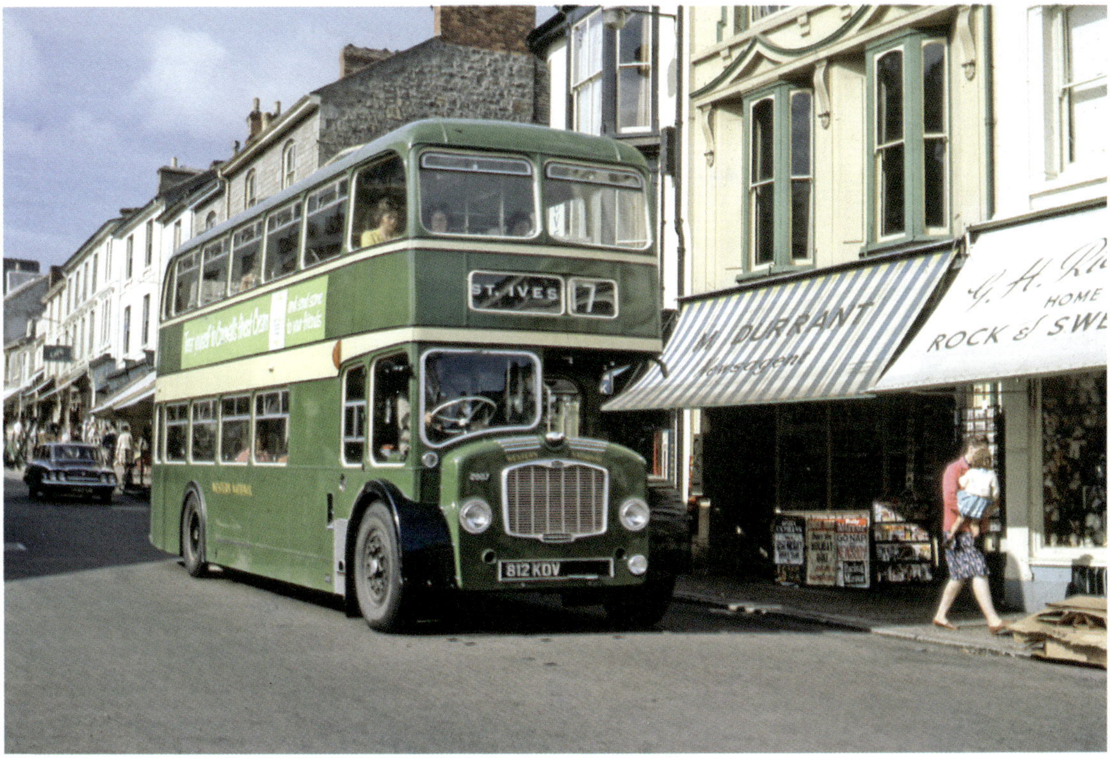
ST. IVES
7
812 KDV
M. DURRANT
Newsagent
HOME
ROCK & SW

The rear-entrance Lodekkas had a less upright frontal profile than did the forward-entrance models, as may be judged by this portrait of West Yorkshire FS6B DX152 (276 BWU) at Harrogate bus station. Other embellishments on this bus which improve its appearance are polished 'whiskers' atop the radiator cowl, and spun-aluminium rear wheel discs. (MSC collection)

Six examples of the 30ft-long, 70-seat rear-entrance FL could be found in the Eastern Counties fleet. LFL59 (559 BPW) was among the last produced, in 1962, after which this model, the least popular of all the Lodekka variants, was deleted. Eastern Counties was Eastern Coach Works' local company operator and purchased more than 260 Lodekkas in total. (G. Lumb)

Bristol Lodekka

The United Counties Omnibus Co, based in Northampton, was among those Tilling-group operators that favoured 'T'-type destination indicators, as fitted to 1965 FS6B No 677 (DNV 677C). It had a 60-seat ECW body with enclosed platform, the manually operated doors being seen here in the closed position. Rear wheel discs are again fitted; these were applied across the Bristol range at this time, and, like similar fittings on contemporary London buses, were a significant visual improvement. (MSC collection)

Hants & Dorset preferred side-by-side destination displays, as exemplified by 70-seat FL6G No 1482 (7682 LJ), its additional length making an interesting comparison with the bus in the previous photograph. Power-operated jack-knife doors are fitted, while the rear wheel disc remains unpainted. (G. Lumb)

Bristol Omnibus and its subsidiary companies received some 560 new Lodekkas – more than 10% of total Lodekka production. Those in the Bristol City fleet received a 'C' prefix to their fleet number, as exemplified by FLF6B No C7136 (829 SHW), loading passengers for Avonmouth, outside the city's bus station in Marlborough Street. From 1965 the company adopted as its fleetname the Bristol scroll – an emblem shared with Bristol Commercial Vehicles and the Bristol Aeroplane Co. (Phil Sposito collection)

Bristol Lodekka

Smartly turned out in Tilling red and cream, Eastern Counties 60-seat FS5G No LFS73 (AAH 173B) heads through Cambridge during September 1971, when seven years old. (Phil Sposito collection)

From 1966, by which time it had been released from the sales restrictions that had hitherto prevented it from selling to operators outside the state-owned sector, BCV gradually introduced new block-letter badging. Notts & Derby (which was closely associated with Midland General) took delivery of this FLF in 1968 as Lodekka production was drawing to a close. No 301 (TRB 568F) displays the new symbols in blue on its wheel hubs, although the scroll remains on the radiator grille. The bus was fitted with Gardner's 6LX engine, which further increased power for Lodekkas. (Phil Sposito collection)

Mansfield District 553 (249 MNN) displays the deep three-piece destination equipment specified by East Midlands operators, providing excellent information for passengers. This vehicle was powered by Bristol's BVW engine, whilst ventilation was provided by a combination of sliding and hopper windows. (Phil Sposito collection)

The FSF model was discontinued in 1963, but four years later Western/Southern National identified a requirement for more vehicles of this type. Twenty such buses were therefore transferred from Bristol Omnibus, including from its Bath Services fleet, 6008 (707 JHY), which was allocated fleet number 1012 by its new owner. Ironically six of these FSFs would return to Bristol Omnibus on 1 January 1970 upon the transfer of Trowbridge and Chippenham services from Western National. (Phil Sposito collection)

Wilts & Dorset followed 38 LDs with 28 rear-entrance FS Lodekkas. Among the latter was 647 (685 AAM), new in 1962, seen racing away from Salisbury city centre at the start of its long journey to Basingstoke. (G. Lumb)

Cheltenham District retained its distinctive livery for more than 20 years after passing to Bristol control, and this readily distinguished its buses from those of the main fleet. Following the formation of NBC Cheltenham's buses shared a similar paint shade with Devon General, although the cream (rather than ivory) relief and its different application around the windows disguised this similarity. FLF6G No 7185 (BHY 715C) displays its Cave-Browne-Cave grilles, as fitted to the vast majority of forward-entrance Lodekkas in the Bristol Omnibus group. (Geoff Gould)

The FLF was easily the most popular of all the F-series models, a total of 1,867 being produced. Brighton Hove & District 75 (FPM 75C) was a 1965 example and another with the larger Gardner engine, being recorded in the chassis register as type FLF6LX. Rear wheel discs again provide the finishing touch to the well-proportioned Bristol/ECW design. For many years BH&D used the same livery as Brighton Corporation, as applied to the vehicle just visible on the right in this view at Brighton station. (Ken Jubb)

Looking resplendent after a repaint, Eastern National FLF No 2705 (85 TVX) displays a mixture of hopper and sliding window ventilators as it stands amongst a group of Lodekkas from the same fleet, while its black window rubbers provide a contrast with the cream fittings on later vehicles. It was, of course, Eastern National FLFs which masqueraded as those of the fictitious Luxton & District Traction Co in the television comedy On The Buses, which ran to seven series. (Phil Sposito collection)

A view inside Bristol Omnibus Company's Gloucester depot, where every vehicle in sight is company-owned. Gloucester's buses carried G-prefix fleet numbers, as in the case of FLF No G7169 (BHU 18C), and displayed the Gloucester coat of arms. From the mid-1960s a gold-block fleetname was also added. (Phil Sposito collection)

Eastern National famously operated a fleet of FLF coaches which included a luggage area at the rear. With an almost full load, 55-seat 2606 (BVX 668B) heads for Irthlingborough, in Northamptonshire, while operating on loan to United Counties. Following the introduction of the new Lodekka cowl, the mesh within the grille was gradually simplified on later models. (MSC collection)

United Automobile 512 (JHN 812D) at Scarborough during 1970, when four years old. An FLF6B, it is fitted with a more modern style of front trafficators, which, it may be noticed, are now positioned further forward in order to be more visible to other road users and to avoid reflecting in the driver's mirrors. On the opposite side of the road is an open-platform FS, also allocated to Scarborough town services. (MSC collection)

From 1965 a slightly longer version of the FLF became available, featuring an extended rear overhang. Such vehicles were more than 31ft long and offered increased capacity, which particularly appealed to Scottish operators. Central SMT BL326 (FGM 326D), an FLF6LX, illustrates the effect of the extra length while standing at Anderston Cross bus station in Glasgow during August 1975. Lower-deck bench seats for five were included, together with additional luggage capacity behind the stairs. (M. S. Curtis)

Scottish Omnibuses AA225 (GSG 225D) was another extra-long FLF6LX, seen displaying the Eastern Scottish fleetname while passengers await departure from Edinburgh's St Andrew Square bus station during the summer of 1975. Constant attention to detail by the Bristol and Eastern Coach Works designers resulted in the lines of the bodywork becoming less complicated over time, with updates such as increased use of glass fibre influencing the elimination of the upper relief band and other unnecessary body detail. (M. S. Curtis)

Every Lodekka was driven as a bare chassis from BCV's works in Brislington to Lowestoft for bodying – a journey of 265 miles. Several chassis are seen here upon arrival at ECW's 'coach factory' during October 1965, that at the centre of the picture being destined for Hants & Dorset. (P. F. Davies)

Taking some 593 examples into stock, Crosville became the largest operator of Bristol Lodekkas, including this 1962 FLF6B. No DFB100 (910 VFM) was among those fitted with an illuminated advertisement panel on the offside, as well as hopper-type window vents. In the background (left) is another Lodekka, convertible LD No DLB977, while on the right is Bristol MW saloon, EMG421. (G. Lumb)

During the summer of 1969 London Transport Routemaster RM1737 was repainted as an overall advertisement for Silexine Paints, a form of advertising never before tried in the UK. One of the first overall-advertisement buses to appear in the provinces was Bristol Omnibus C7109 (802 SHW), an FLF6B, which late in 1971 was painted red (in contrast to Tilling green) to promote Berni Inns. Many more overall advertisements have followed, but none has matched the impact achieved by the first examples. (John May)

Sister vehicle C7133 (826 SHW) also received a special livery, in May 1971. Bristol Omnibus was at this time introducing a revised livery, with more cream, for one-man-operated vehicles, and as an experiment this crew-operated FLF was repainted in a similar style. However, less than a month later the bus had its green areas repainted again, this time in London Country's Lincoln green. Thus adorned, it is seen approaching the bus wash at the Bristol company's Lawrence Hill depot. (Bristol Omnibus Co)

ABOVE Crosville was another operator to purchase FLF coaches, these incorporating extra luggage space at the rear, as well as ventilators of railway-carriage pattern. DFB150 (AFM 113B) heads towards Cemaes Bay on the Isle of Anglesey, on its long journey across North Wales from Liverpool. (MSC collection)

OPPOSITE TOP Following the creation of the National Bus Company large numbers of Lodekkas were drafted into the West Riding fleet from sister NBC subsidiaries. West Riding had been an ardent supporter of the Guy Wulfrunian double-decker, which proved unsuccessful, and the type's withdrawal was expedited by the introduction of the Lodekkas. Among the first to arrive was former Lincolnshire 2301 (KFW 312), a 1954 LD6G, which took fleet number 422. (Phil Sposito collection)

OPPOSITE BOTTOM Another operator to be allocated the Lodekka second-hand in NBC days was East Midland Motor Services, its acquisition of a lone example resulting in the application of yet another livery style. No D75 (975 ARA) was an LD6G, previously numbered 456 in the Midland General fleet. It was photographed at Retford during July 1971. (Phil Sposito collection)

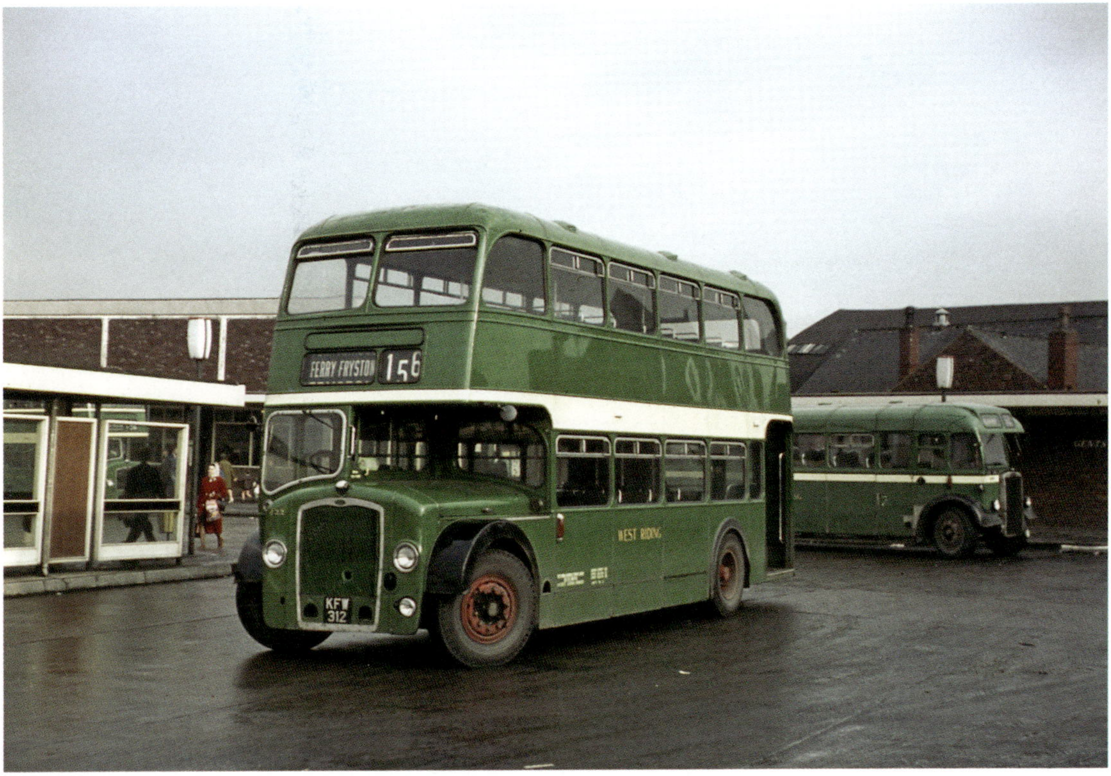
FERRY FRYSTON 156
WEST RIDING
KFW 312

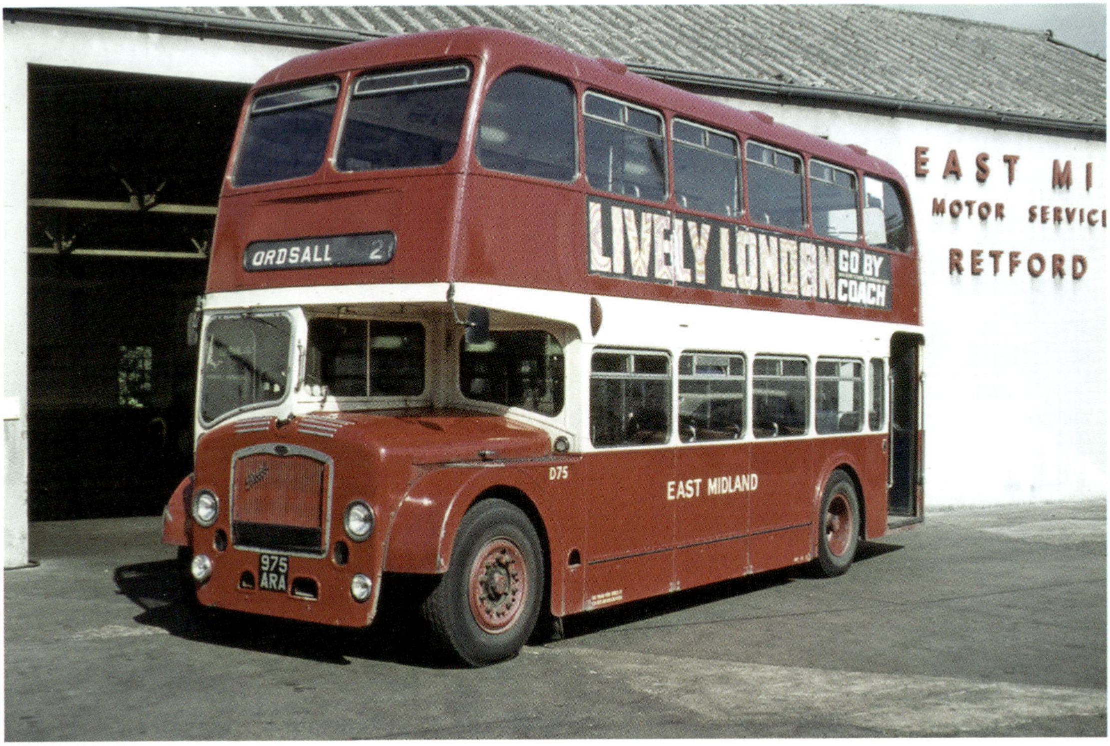
ORDSALL 2
LIVELY LONDON GO BY COACH
EAST MIDLAND
D75
975 ARA
RETFORD

The final FLF Lodekkas for Bristol Omnibus were perhaps the best looking, with much simplified body detail, glass-fibre rear wheel discs, a single waistband and the omission of the Cave-Browne-Cave air intakes. They were also received in a slightly different shade of Tilling green, with a pale cream band. Having joined the fleet during 1967, Bristol-engined C7311 (KHW 303E) waits time at the Broomhill terminus of route 5. (Bristol Vintage Bus Group)

The last of 5,217 Bristol Lodekkas to be built materialised as Midland General 313 (YNU 351G), an FLF6G delivered during September 1968. One of a relatively small number of FLFs to be fitted with semi-automatic transmission, it is seen alongside 1958 LD6G No 476 (261 HNU). (G. Lumb)

Bristol Lodekka

With rear-engined buses becoming more popular during the 1960s and one-man operation gaining acceptance, Bristol looked to develop a successor to the Lodekka which conformed to these trends while continuing to take advantage of the Lodekka's low overall height. During September 1966 Bristol revealed its longitudinal-engined VR, which, with ECW bodywork, displayed a strong family resemblance to the final FLFs. During that month prototype VRX.002 (HHW 933D) was posed in Gypsy Lane, Keynsham. This isolated location is almost unchanged today and, by a curious coincidence, now forms the approach to Bath Bus Company's depot. (MSC collection)

When Bristol VR production commenced in 1968, a transverse-engined variant – the VRT – became by far the more popular choice among operators. This model was promoted in company publicity as 'Another winner from the Lodekka stable' and was selected by most Lodekka users for future double-deck requirements. Bristol Omnibus itself immediately ordered 28 but cancelled these at the last moment in favour of RELL single-deckers. The nearest early VRTs to the Bristol works were therefore to be found working for Western National in Bridgwater (some 30 miles southwest of the city), among them Nos 1051/5 (OTA 285/9G) seen here. (MSC collection)

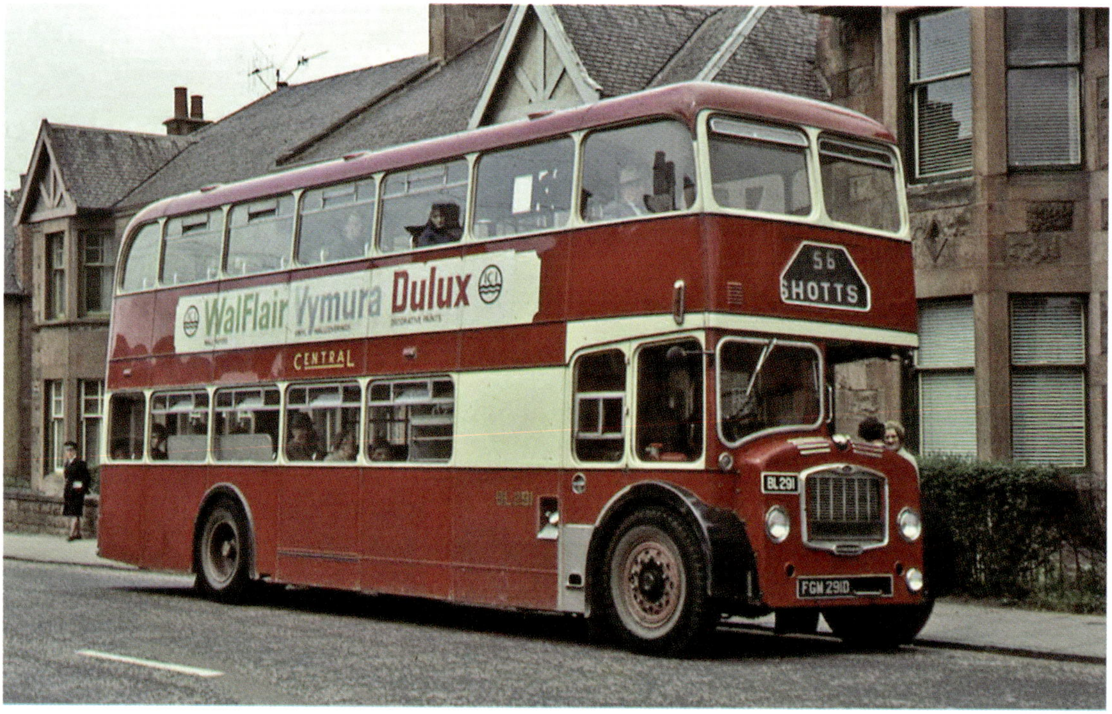
56
SHOTTS
WalFlair Vymura Dulux
CENTRAL
BL 291
FGM 291D

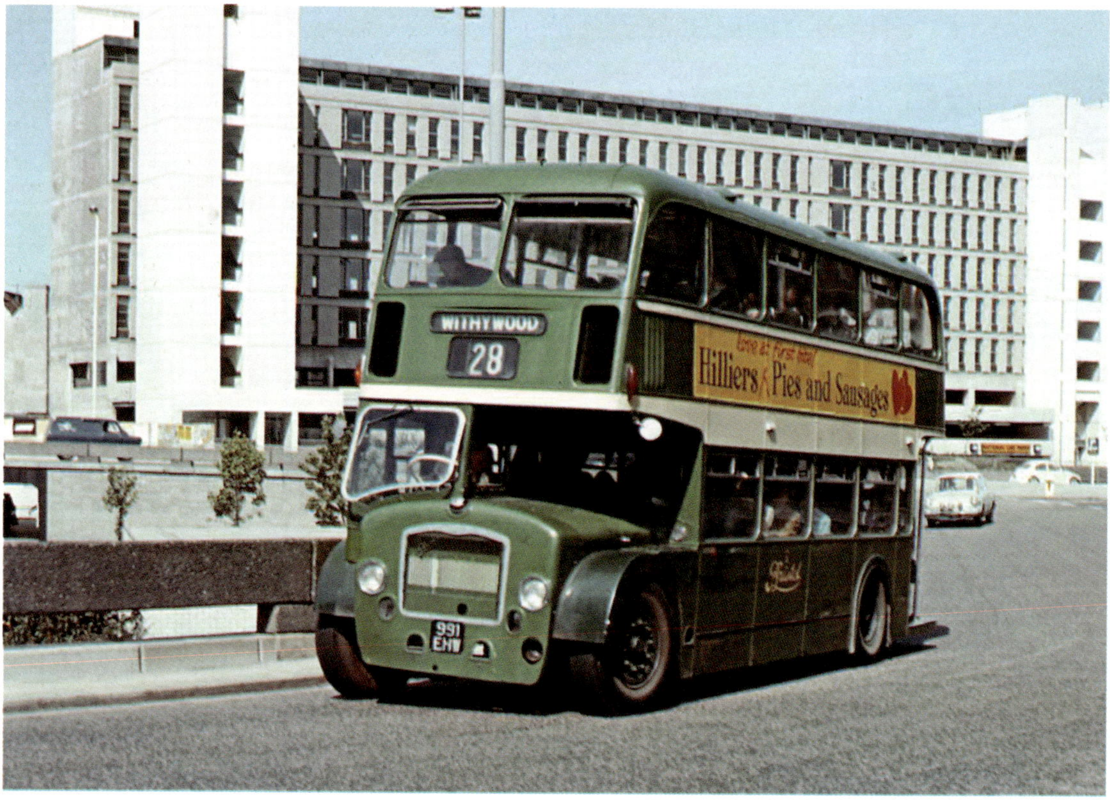
WITHYWOOD
28
Hilliers Pies and Sausages
991 EHW

OPPOSITE TOP Central SMT FLF No BL291 (FGM 291D) shows to good advantage the extra-long rear overhang of its 31ft-long body, with bench seat for five passengers over the wheel arch. Its fleetname is of the original style applied, while the position chosen for this was unusual among bus operators at the time. (Phil Sposito collection)

OPPOSITE BOTTOM Travelling at speed around the St James Barton roundabout in Bristol during the summer of 1972 is Bristol Omnibus LD6B No LC8534 (991 EHW), its hinged windscreen open to provide additional ventilation for the driver. For passengers, push-out upper-deck vents also improved airflow, although this batch, with a limited number of hoppers included within the side windows, suffered from poor top-deck ventilation generally. (Phil Sposito collection)

ABOVE In order to overcome the sales restrictions imposed on Bristol and ECW agreement was reached with Dennis whereby the latter would build the Lodekka under licence as the Loline, allowing the model to be sold to operators outside the state-owned sector. 465 FRB, a 30ft-long Loline with 70-seat Willowbrook body, was built in 1958 for Tailby & George (Blue Bus Service), which fleet was absorbed by Derby Corporation in 1973. It is seen wearing Derby livery as No 32. (MSC collection)

Flat-floor Lolines were introduced with the Mk II model. Fitted with 74-seat bodywork by Willowbrook, Gardner 6LW-powered 248 HDH joined the Walsall Corporation fleet in 1960 as No 848. In this view it continues to display its original fleet number but has West Midlands fleetnames, the Walsall undertaking having been among those combined in 1969 to form West Midlands PTE. (MSC collection)

Bristol Lodekka

North Western Road Car Co was a strong supporter of Bristol-built vehicles before nationalisation restricted their supply. The purchase of Dennis Lolines was therefore a natural alternative, 50 being added to the fleet. Pictured in Manchester during September 1970 is No 892 (RDB 892), a 1962 Loline III with Gardner 6LX engine and 71-seat Alexander body. (Phil Sposito collection)

ABOVE During 1972 North Western's bus operations were divided between the recently formed SELNEC PTE, Crosville and Trent. As a consequence the Lolines passed to new owners, RDB 897 joining many Lodekkas in the Crosville fleet. Shortly before the introduction of NBC standard liveries Crosville had adopted a much lighter shade of green, as applied to this vehicle, another Loline III with Alexander body, by now numbered DEG402. (MSC collection)

RIGHT Reading Transport took three batches of Loline IIIs, the last entering service early in 1967, by which time Bristol was again able to trade freely. Among them was 79 (GRD 579D), with 68-seat East Lancs bodywork, seen descending Station Hill. These buses incorporated Bristol gearboxes and rear axles, the latter even displaying the Bristol scroll on their hubs! In later years Reading would standardise on Bristol's RE and VRT models. (MSC collection)

Bristol Lodekka

Bristol Lodekka

By far the most important customer for the Loline was Dennis's local bus operator, Aldershot & District, which took 141 into stock. Here an Alexander-bodied Loline III new to A&D is seen heading through picturesque Chiddingfold in July 1975. By this time NBC had dictated the merger of several subsidiaries, Aldershot & District having amalgamated with Thames Valley on 1 January 1972; still in traditional colours, one time A&D 455 (455 EOT) now bears fleet number 797 and Alder Valley fleetnames. (MSC collection)

Bristol Lodekka

Brighton Hove & District was absorbed by Southdown, resulting in one of the few instances whereby an NBC-inspired merger didn't detract from the appearance of the vehicles involved – not that BH&D colours were unattractive. Having arrived at the terminus of the one-time trolleybus service from Hollingbury, the driver leaps from the cab of ex-BH&D FSF No 2031 (VAP 31), the latter by now in full apple green and cream, with Southdown BH&D fleetnames in the short-lived style introduced in the early 1970s. Clearly visible is the illuminated offside advertisement panel, a feature specified on many Lodekkas when fluorescent lighting was introduced to interiors. (Phil Sposito collection)

Initially NBC planned to offer a range of around half-a-dozen shades as the basis of liveries for its subsidiaries, and from among these Alder Valley selected dark red. Later, however, the choice of colours was reduced, but among buses to receive the dark red was FLF No 604 (UJB 203), one of a batch of five, new to Thames Valley in 1960, which were the only forward-entrance Lodekkas (apart from the prototypes) to feature a sliding entrance door. (MSC collection)

By the end of 1972 the full ramifications of NBC's corporate livery policy had become apparent, traditional colours and fleetname styles being replaced by leaf green or poppy red in all but a handful of exceptional cases. Demonstrating the new standard green livery, with white waistband and grey wheels, is Lincolnshire FL6G No 2701 (OVL 485). At least this operator, unlike many, continued to paint Lodekka mudguards black. (MSC collection)

The red version of NBC's corporate livery applied to another FL6G, L1460 (14 AAX) in the fleet of Red & White Services. It was photographed at the company's Bulwark works, Chepstow, during August 1975. Red & White was the largest operator of the FL-type Lodekka, with 20. (M. S. Curtis)

In order to promote its new corporate identity NBC decided to mount a television advertising campaign during October/November 1972. This involved 50 buses from different subsidiaries assembling at a military base in Aldershot, where they were filmed displaying the new fleetnames and colours – including from the air, the buses being driven in formation to create the double-N symbol! Bristol's contribution was FLF Lodekka C7211 (DHW 991C), which emerged from the paint shops complete with new-style fleetnames, a white waistband and grey wheels. However, as the company had yet to adopt NBC leaf green the bus was turned out in Tilling green, with Brunswick-green wings! This photograph shows it freshly outshopped at Lawrence Hill. (M. Walker)

As repainting entire fleets of buses would take at least two years to complete, attempts were made to add features of the new NBC liveries to existing colour schemes, although ironically this probably made the organisation appear more fragmented than was actually the case. New in 1963 as Brighton Hove & District No 56, FS6G Lodekka 4656 AP is seen some 10 years later as Southdown 2056, with the inevitable grey wheels and with Southdown-BH&D fleetnames, in NBC corporate style, applied to traditional Brighton colours. (MSC collection)

Crosville operated the largest fleet of Bristol Lodekkas, with 593 purchased new. Among them was this Gardner-engined 60-seat FS, No DFG184 (EFM 633C), with enclosed platform and hopper window vents, which, photographed from this angle, provides an interesting comparison with the Southern National LD shown on page 16. From 1978 the NBC symbol was applied in red and blue on a rectangular white background, which went some way towards brightening the livery. (MSC collection)

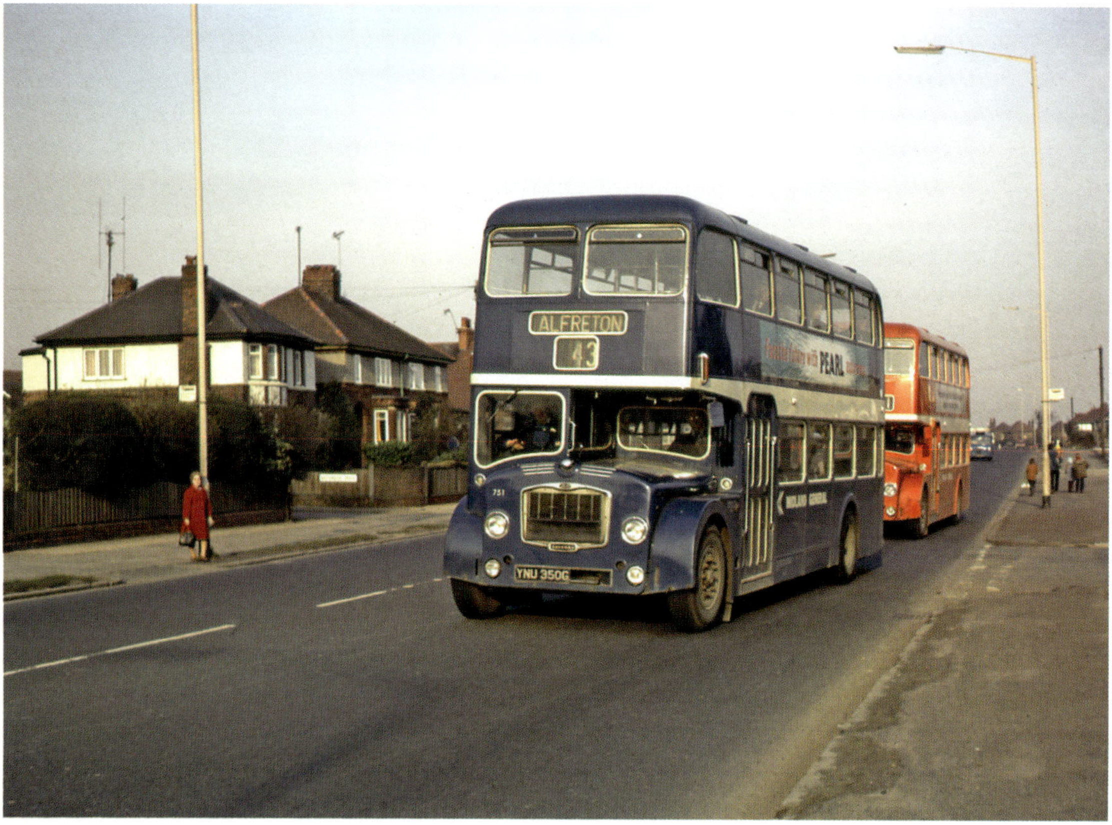
ALFRETON
43
PEARL
YNU 350G

SAUSAGES
Spear's
AND PIES
Bristol

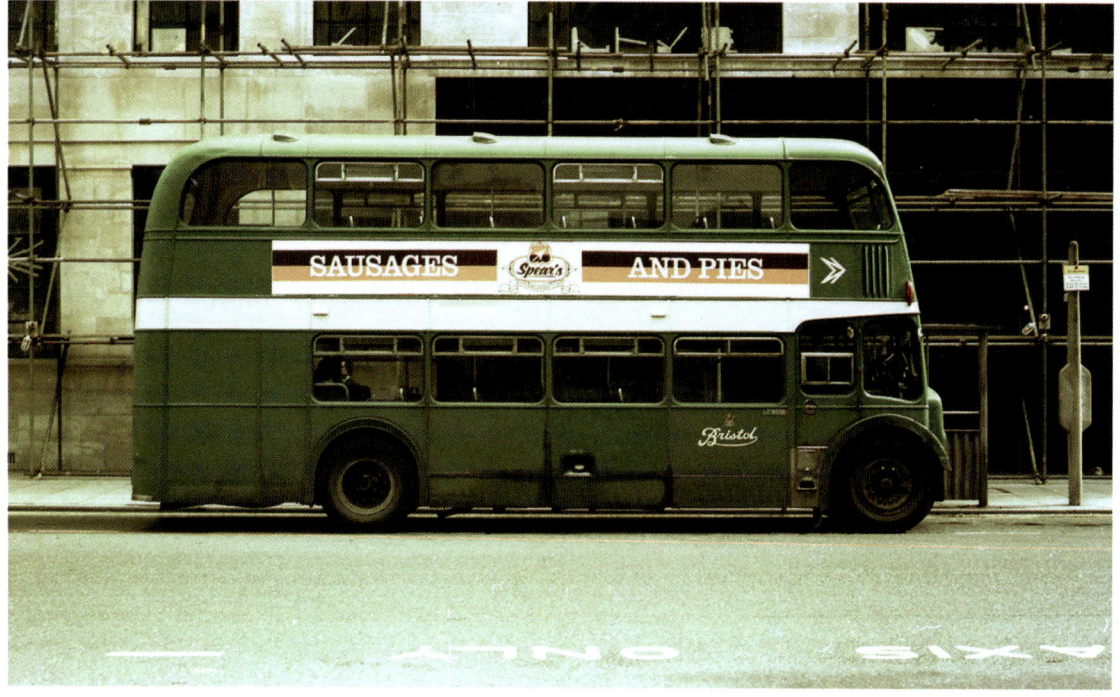

OPPOSITE TOP Several NBC subsidiaries clung desperately to blue livery, but in almost every case they were forced to switch to poppy red. Among them was Midland General, which initially repainted buses in its standard blue but with white waistband, as exemplified by late-model semi-automatic FLF6LX No 751 (YNU 350G), bound for Alfreton. It is pursued by an earlier FLF which has already succumbed to the poppy-red treatment. (Phil Sposito collection)

OPPOSITE BOTTOM A number of operators deviated from NBC's corporate livery policy when the opportunity arose. In the Lodekka's home city the Bristol company managed the fleet which was half-owned by the Corporation, so, following the introduction of standardised liveries, city buses (slowly) adopted leaf green but with a new white scroll surmounted by the city's coat-of-arms and with the double-N symbol above the driver's cab. Unfortunately, pressure to adopt the new style before scheduled repainting caused many buses to take on a shabby appearance. Pictured in 1974, 15 year-old LD No LC8519 (973 EHW), still in Tilling green, has had its upper cream band overpainted green and its lower band repainted white, while the yellow scroll has been obliterated and the white version applied further forward. Its grey wheels and much of the body remain covered in road dirt. (M. S. Curtis)

ABOVE Eastern National was another operator to retain black wings on Lodekkas and went to great lengths to maintain smart grey wheels. Several Lodekkas feature in this scene at Clacton bus station, where an NBC flag has been raised to reinforce the corporate image. Nearest the camera is FLF6B No 2720 (801 WVW). (MSC collection)

Western National daringly deviated from NBC standard layout with increased areas of white on three of its FLF buses. No 2044 (ATA 125B) had previously worn an attractive livery of cream with green trim, for services along the North Cornwall coast, and the new application represented an attempt to maintain a special livery following the introduction of NBC's corporate image. (MSC collection)

Bristol Lodekka

On the grounds of saving costs NBC encouraged operators to dispense with the white relief band when repainting vehicles. Crosville was among several companies to adopt this idea, which it extended to painting the entire bodywork in NBC green, including grille surround, mudguards and illuminated advertisement panel. The effect was appalling, as demonstrated by 1960 FS6G No DFG38 (319 PFM), the spartan appearance of which can have done little to encourage passenger travel. (MSC collection)

ABOVE During the Tilling era open-top buses operating at coastal resorts had traditionally been painted cream, but in order to comply with the NBC corporate image introduced in the early 1970s some operators tried all-over white for such vehicles. The result was far less appealing, as demonstrated by Crosville DLG813 (XFM 225), a 1956 Gardner-engined LD with convertible-open-top bodywork, at Aberystwyth. (Phil Sposito collection)

OPPOSITE TOP The Scottish Bus Group steadfastly resisted standard liveries but would eventually accede to the introduction of corporate fleetnames. Alexander (Fife)'s bright-red FS6G No FRD175 (3661 FG) was seemingly being tailed by the Police when photographed on a misty day in May 1978. (MSC collection)

OPPOSITE BOTTOM Motherwell-based Central SMT was the largest Scottish operator of Lodekkas purchased new, taking some 355 examples. Six are lined up here at Hamilton, all with shortened front wings. From left to right are FLFs BE231/2/0 and BE176, 31ft FLF BL281 and FS B194. (MSC collection)

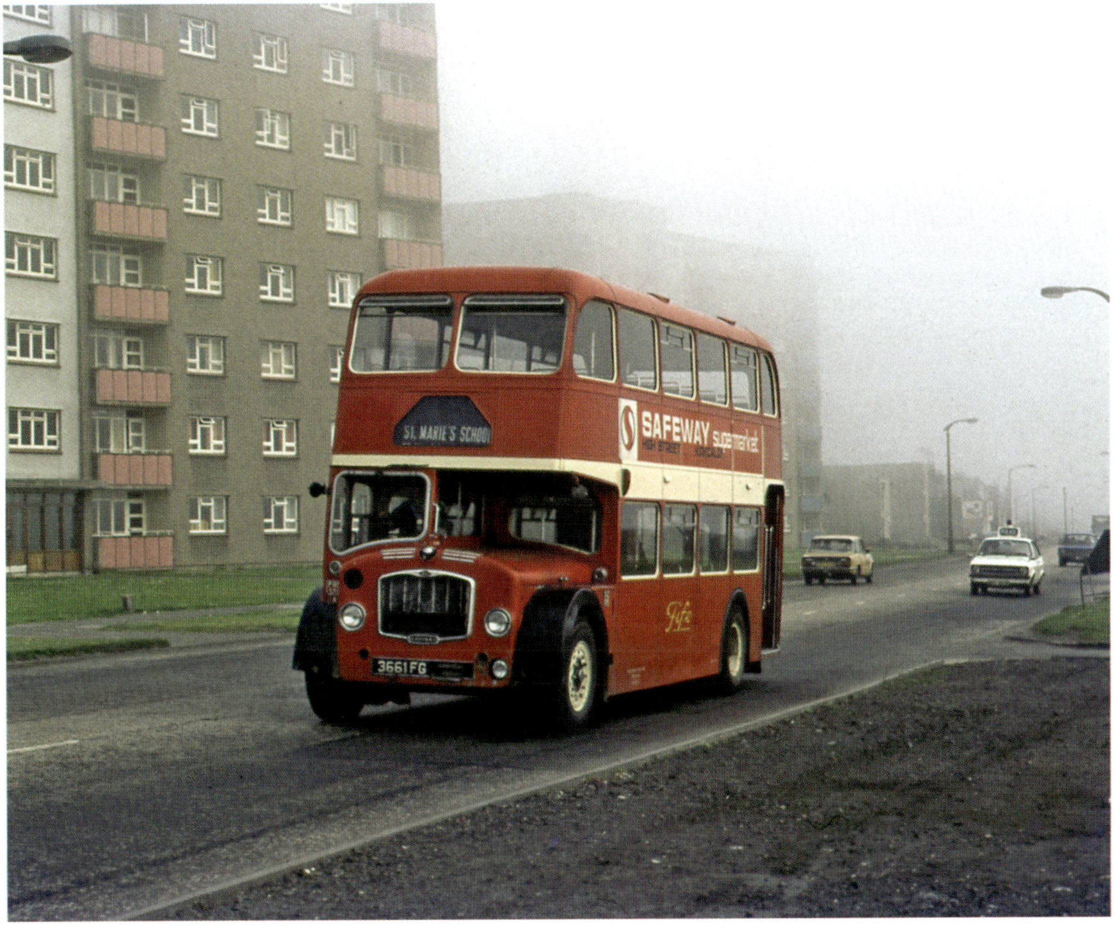
SAFEWAY supermarket
3661 FG
Fife

HAMILTON

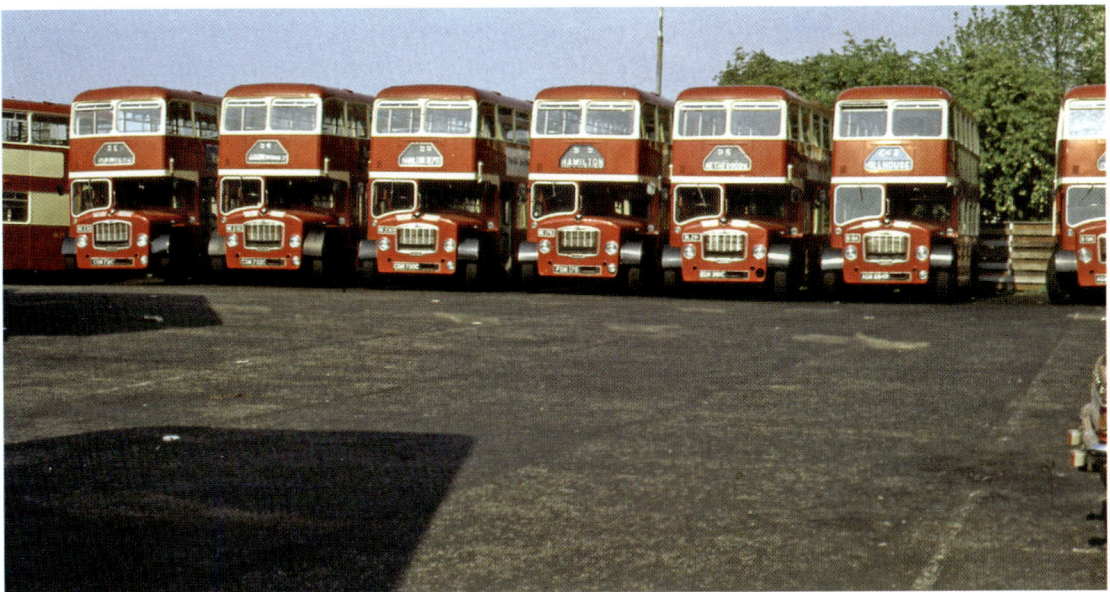

During the early 1970s no fewer than 106 of its newest FLF Lodekkas were exchanged by NBC for early Bristol VRTs with Scottish operators. The Scottish group was discouraged by the relative unreliability of rear-engined buses, while NBC was seeking to convert services to one-man operation as rapidly as possible. The reliability of Lodekkas therefore appealed to the likes of Western SMT, which company's B2440 (PBL 59F) had previously been Alder Valley 691. It is seen Glasgow's Anderston Cross bus station in August 1975, with an inverted triangular destination screen. (M. S. Curtis)

Further colour was added to the Scottish transport scene by Alexander (Northern)'s use of a yellow-and-cream livery. Sporting Northern Scottish fleetnames in corporate style, NRD5 (UEV 221E) was another bus involved in the NBC/SBG exchanges, having originally been Eastern National 2883. However, it reached Northern – which, having no VRTs, had not been involved in the exchanges – in 1979, as one of a group of five FLFs transferred within SBG from Alexander (Midland). (Phil Sposito collection)

Once its passenger-carrying career was over Bristol Omnibus FLF6G No 7158 (AAE 263B) became a driver-training vehicle, given new number W175 in the Works series and with staircase removed to create a position for the instructor behind the driver, in which form it was allocated to the company's Lawrence Hill driving school. The blue livery for driver-training vehicles was introduced in 1974 by a new General Manager, Richard Roberts, who had transferred from Eastern National, where a similar livery was applied to the training fleet. (MSC collection)

Another FLF (this time with Gardner 6LX engine) to be relegated to training duties was JNU 987D, which had started life as Midland General 663 but after withdrawal in 1978 became No 104 in the United Automobile training fleet. (MSC collection)

ABOVE A different role lay in store for a number of Lodekkas, including several Western SMT LDs that were converted into towing wagons at the end of their passenger-carrying careers. No W7027 (with trade plate 0024 HS) stands ready for its next call at Inchinnan in 1978. (MSC collection)

OPPOSITE TOP After withdrawal by state-owned operators many Lodekkas found their way into the fleets of independents. OK Motor Services, of Bishop Auckland, ran this 70-seat FLF6B for four years. New to Bristol Omnibus as C7134, 827 SHW moved to the North East in 1977 when 13 years old. (Phil Sposito collection)

OPPOSITE BOTTOM Many Lodekkas were exported at the end of their operational lives in normal public service. In Dordrecht, Holland, Peter van der Merwe's fleet included FLF 03-MB-85 (left), formerly Western SMT B1951, and (right) 40-03-ZB, a 31ft-long FLF new as Eastern National 2900. They were photographed on an enthusiasts' tour in 2001, when another member of this fleet to be encountered was 96-87-EB, originally West Yorkshire DX2, one of the pre production LDs of 1953 and by now the oldest surviving Lodekka. (M. Walker)

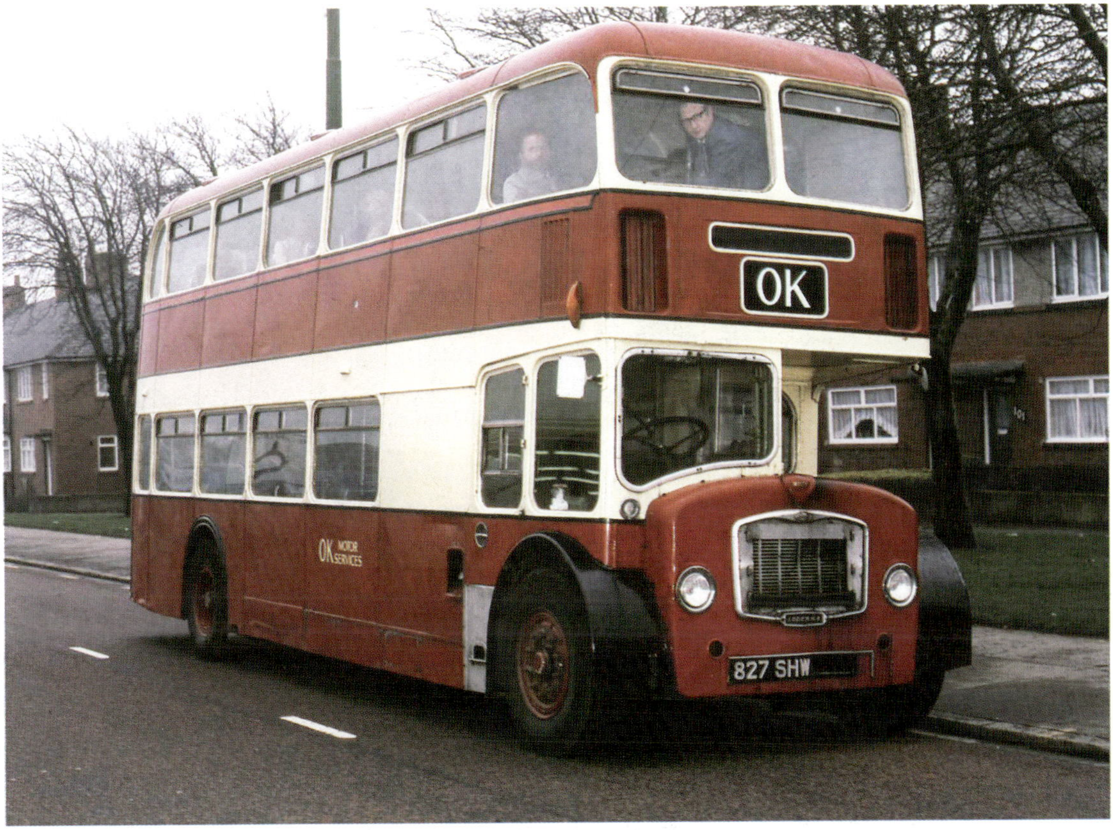
OK
OK MOTOR SERVICES
827 SHW

van de MERWE Oldtimers Dordrecht
LONDON BUS
03 MB-85
48-03-ZB

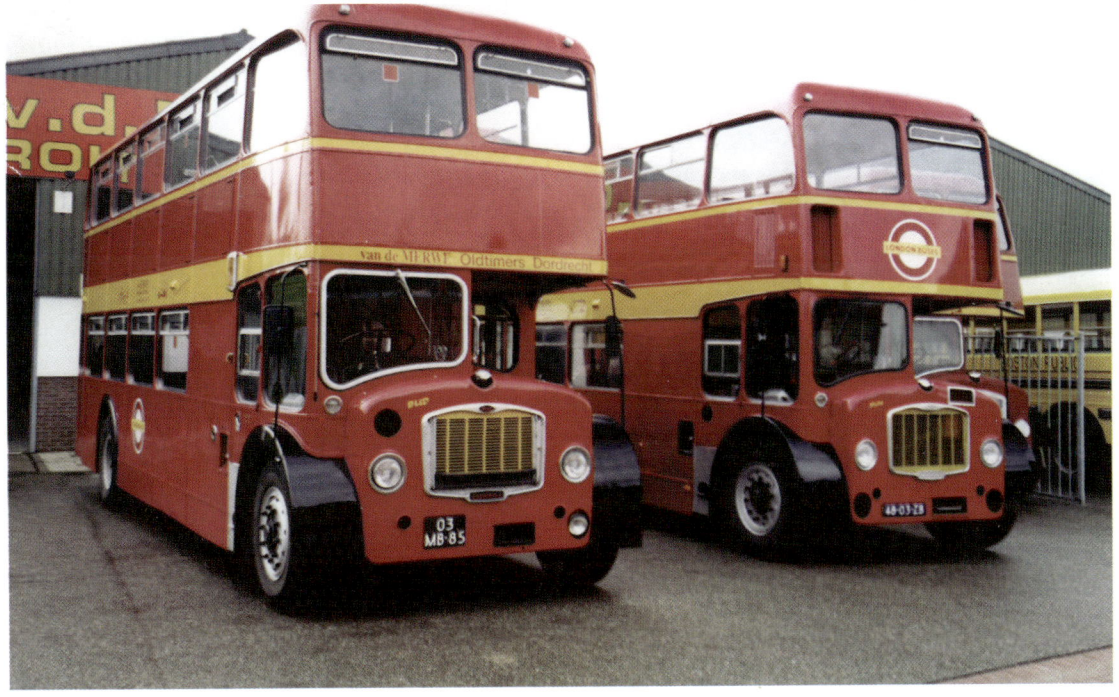

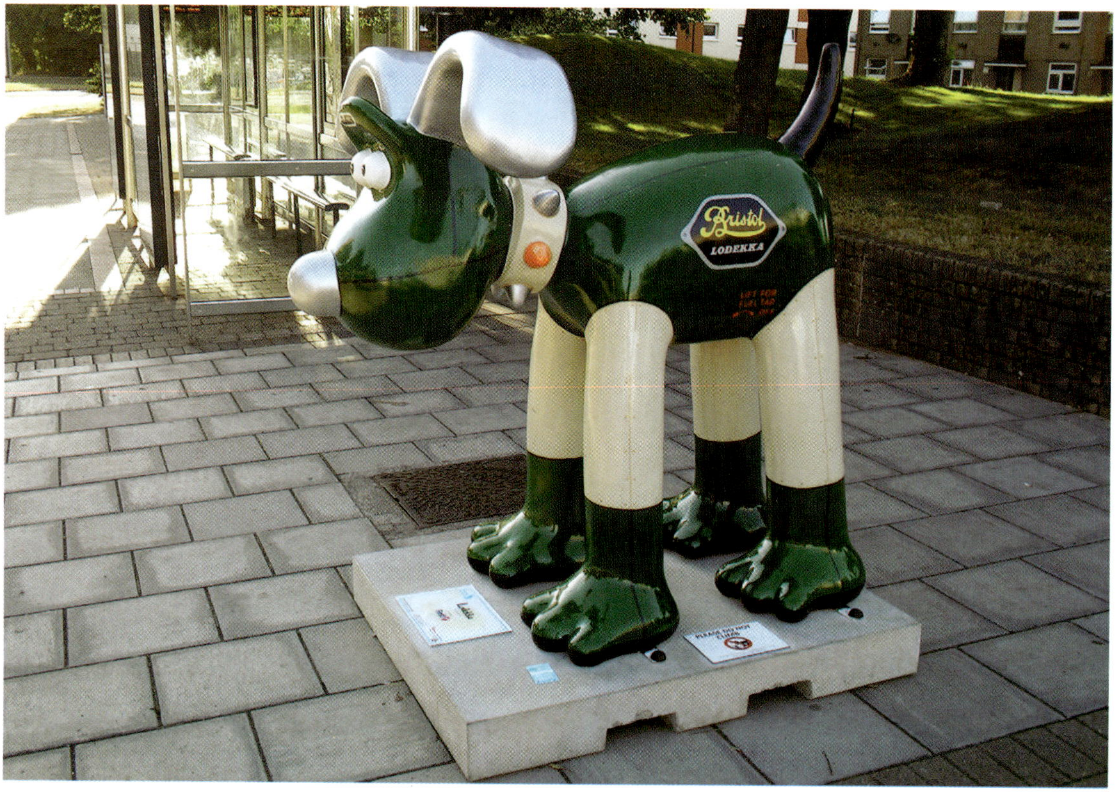

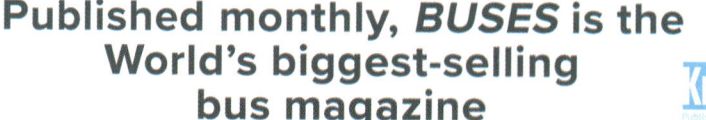

The TV and film characters Wallace and Gromit are created in Bristol. During the summer of 2013 no fewer than 80 large glass-fibre replicas of Gromit were displayed in and around the city as part of a 'Gromit Unleashed' public art exhibition, staged to support Bristol Children's Hospital charity. Each was decorated with a particular theme, and to its credit, First organised and sponsored a Lodekka Gromit, which was positioned near the company's Lawrence Hill depot. (M. S. Curtis)

Published monthly, *BUSES* is the World's biggest-selling bus magazine

KEY Publishing

Visit: **www.keybuses.com** for more details

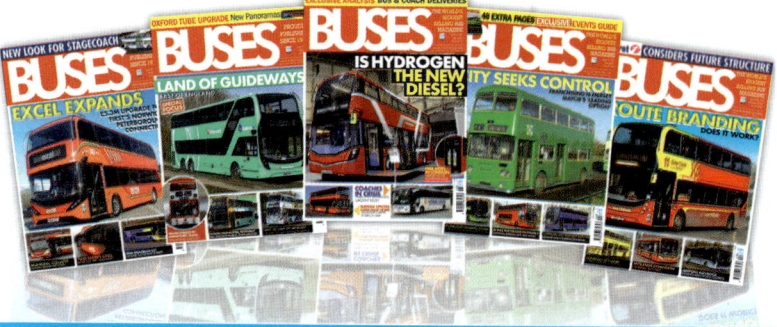